T0062488

Around the Block in America

Rose Michiko Sato Stults

authorHOUSE®

AuthorHouse™
1663 Liberty Drive
Bloomington, IN 47403
www.authorhouse.com
Phone: 1-800-839-8640

©2012 Rose Michiko Sato Stults. All rights reserved.

No part of this book may be reproduced, stored in a retrieval system, or transmitted by any means without the written permission of the author.

First published by AuthorHouse 1/2/2013

ISBN: 978-1-4520-1335-0 (sc)
ISBN: 978-1-4520-1336-7 (e)

Library of Congress Control Number: 2010905965

Printed in the United States of America
Bloomington, Indiana

This book is printed on acid-free paper.

This book is dedicated to
the Sato Family

The last birthday before his passing 1977.
Masamori Sato, born December 1, 1885
and passed April 8, 1978

Acknowledgements

I'd like to dedicate my book in the memory of my father Masamori Sato. As a young impoverished man in the latter 1800's, he grew up in Kagoshima, Japan. He had so much tenacity and strong will that ultimately became the blessing to us all in our family.

My blessing also includes the many folks who have affected me along my life's journey that has prompted me to leave behind this legacy for posterity.

I very much appreciated the special kindness and help that my older brother John and sister Betty have shown me from childhood and on...

Also, I'd like to extend credit to my brother's Bob and Frank for their family compilations. It helped me to be able to extract information that also includes Betty's "Exhibit A" transcript.

Kindness prevailed in the least most unexpected place. I met Margretta Mueller an English major at a health food store whose diligence really enhanced and gave color to my story. Kay Heck and Kendra Rand of the English Department at Walter State Community College in Tennessee helped me by deciphering my hand written script into the "First Edited Draft." Roger Besch's professionalism was also very helpful with the photo's...., especially the one on the cover.

Finally, this is for my two wonderful adopted children, Andy Gene Stults and Jennifer Lynn Stults who knows so very little about their Japanese Ancestry and heritage.

Contents

Chapter I

Family History of Masamori and Masuyo Sato formerly of Sumner, Washington

Japan is a caste system society where the oldest son is the most highly regarded person after the father in the family and in the society. They have a code of ethics with many unwritten and unsaid laws of do's and don'ts, doctor's are only paid if the patients stay well.

This is the story about my father Masamori Sato. He was born in Kagoshima, Japan on December 1, 1885. He was a descendant of a samurai family.

The history of Japan in the formative time was unpopulated with rich vegetation and a wonderful tropical climate. People from Korea were the first to walk across the land bridge known today as the Japan Sea. They migrated to the south most sector of Japan known today as Kyushu. Eventually, the Chinese walked across the land bridge to migrate directly eastward to the central part of Honshu and Kyushu. Finally, the Russians went across the land bridge to the northerly most Hokkaido sector of Japan. The northerner's have the distinction of having a very fair complexion and a much taller stature than the rest of the countrymen.

The earliest immigrants were often defended by the stronger men in their midst who became the leaders like "Robin Hood." These leader's developed more followers' who supported them in defending the defenseless. As more leaders and followers developed they sometimes became at odds with each other, then there would be war. This began the samurai era in the southern and central part of Japan. The leaders in each group became the warlord and his followers' became the samurai. The warlord's were very instructive in building large castles in high elevated locations surrounded by high walls with sentries posted to look for any enemy. Only the samurai and their families were privileged to reside in the castles and to receive education for their children. The peasants were considered to be inferior, and lived outside the castles. They did all the hard labor growing rice and soybeans, while many of the men went fishing for their mainstay protein in their diet. The children did not receive any education.

The men were only about 4 1/2 feet tall as judged by the manikins, dressed in full armor and encased in glass cases in a museum. The original armor used in their time of war is still displayed showing racks and racks of heavy and very awkward looking swords that are still mounted along many walls where they were from the late eighteenth century in Kyoto, Japan. One castle was built on the cliffs edge in Kyoto has structural tree poles at various lengths that are as much as 40 feet in length supporting the overhanging section of the castle on the cliff's edge. This was an engineering feat at the time when the man in charge insisted that only a certain kind of tree be used to withstand the test of time. The tree used for the support was the su (pronounced soo) tree. Today, these supports hardly look blemished and are in remarkable condition.

When the samurai era ended, they all dispersed forming various villages, and they became more civil. The former samurai started to educate the peasant children. My great, great, grandfather was the first to begin teaching the village children in his home. As more and more peasant parents wanted education for their children, there was not enough room for him to facilitate them all. So, the village folks decided to build the first formal school in southern Japan. Gradually, the first children who attended were able to mentor the other children. They became instrumental in the teaching and education process.

The Youthful Years

Masamori was the fourth generation descendant of a samurai family. In his younger days, he walked 4 or 5 miles to school often without shoes because of the poor economic times of the whole country. It made him tough, and he learned to work hard. In his youth, he even worked in a very laborious gold mine that today is open to viewers as a museum. It has depictions of the various kinds of work men had to do while the mine was in operation.

He received a rich education through home teaching, a very useful blessing though his family was poor financially. In those days, he was an avid reader. Then one day, he read about a country that believed in "Equality and Justice for All." This knowledge came at a very meaningful and a critical time that became a turning point in his life. It helped that he was a young and adventuresome spirit, and he now envisioned traveling to that distant land.

Masamori was one of four boys in his family. In a caste system society, the number one son has always been the most highly esteemed member of a family after the father. So, as the third son, he detested his low ranking status and became self-motivated to go to this newfound land that really excited him. He wanted to become his own man with a yardstick to use in his own personal life.

Testing his Father's Work Ethics

At the age of 15, he left home setting out into the unknown world. He needed a trade that would further his life's burning goal. He set his sights on a brilliant idea of going to the port of Hiroshima, Japan. There, he hoped for the possibility of employment at the shipyard to begin learning to navigate a ship traveling to America.

When he reached the seaport of Hiroshima, he was hired as a maintenance worker to paint the exterior of the ships. Each morning, he was given the proper tools to do his assigned job. There were many days of grueling work as taskmasters kept everyone in tow. One day when he accidentally dropped his tool in the deep water at the dock, the penalty for such carelessness meant that he would be docked pay at the end of the day. His diligence and perseverance helped him to advance to a more responsible level of work to become a "Swabby." Next, he was assigned to a ship that guarded the coastal waters of Japan.

These ships went to various ports such as to China, Korea, Vladivostok, Russia, in Siberia. When these ships docked at these seaports, most of the men herded to the local bars. Masamori usually spent his time educating himself on the important aspects of boat navigation at the local libraries. If the navigator of the ship was available, he would get firsthand knowledge from him. The captain of the ship often warned all the shipmate's to be cautious of eating unaccustomed foods in these countries. So, one day while venturing out into the countryside, he became very hungry and came upon a banana plantation. The men were inviting him to eat what they had, but because he didn't recognize their fruit, he was very reluctant to try it. Then he remembered his captain's warning, but when they peeled the fruit eating only the inside, he concluded that it couldn't be contaminated and was safe to eat. They soon convinced him to try some.

When he tasted the fruit, he was pleasantly surprised how good it tasted and enjoyed them immensely. So, then he decided to introduce his shipmates to his exciting experience. He then took a huge rack of bananas back to the ship with him; they all enjoyed them as much as he did. He was a hero to have tried this untried food and they praised him for his adventuresome spirit.

American Arrival

Then, one day when he became confident enough that he was capable of navigating a big cargo passenger ship, he was rewarded with an assignment to the NYK (Nippon Yusen Kaisha) line ship that made voyages to the United States of America. In those days, it took two months for ships to reach the new land that he would learn to love and call his home. When the ship reached Tacoma, Washington and docked, he jumped ship and entered this country without a passport.

He soon was harbored by the earlier arrivals from Japan who were operating laundry, restaurants, and hotel businesses. When the captain of the ship discovered him missing, there was an all out search to find him; he was hunted by the local authorities to be shot on site for the two weeks that the ship was in the harbor. It was a very critical issue for the captain of the ship who then had to navigate the ship back to Japan himself. The immediate disadvantage was the language barrier as a new arrival to this land. The Japanese businesses were eager to hire him for pittance while working him long and laborious hours at a sawmill near Tacoma, on the railroad near Three Forks, Montana, then Othello, Washington, and on the Yamada farm in Firwood, near Puyallup, Washington. By being very frugal, he was able to save towards leasing a farm with another Japanese bachelor. He was later able to manage a trip back home to Japan.

Proud Father's Welcome

He was excitedly welcomed home by his father who was so proud of his accomplishment that when dinnertime came, his oldest brother lost his high ranking seating position next to his father at the dinner table for Masamori.

With the excitement of Masamori's homecoming, his father even made wedding arrangements for Masamori unbeknown to him. He quickly renounced his father's plans. He didn't appreciate the injustice shown to this older brother, because these were the very reasons why he left the caste system society in Japan in the first place. (However, according to the records in Japan, he was married twice instead of once.)

New Neighbors and Marriage

After returning to the farm in Firwood, Washington, there were now new neighbors farming next to him. Mr. Takijiro Ishikawa was from Japan. He had worked on a sugar plantation in Hawaii soon after the death of his wife, while leaving his two daughters in the care of their maternal grandparents. Mr. Ishikawa then left Hawaii and headed for the United States of America, and settled on the farm in Firwood, Washington adjoining Masamori's farm. When he was able, he sent passage money to the lady that he had met in Hawaii and also his two daughters in Japan to join him in America, and then he married Tsuru Sato.

Once Mr. Ishikawa met Masamori, he wanted to know more about him, so he returned to Japan to meet with his family. He was so pleased when he learned that he was a descendant of a samurai family in Kagoshima, Japan, a town in southern Kyusu, Japan. It was considered a highly honorable genealogy lineage in Japan even today! He then approached Masamori to see if he would be interested in marrying his oldest daughter Masuyo, and he was very receptive. Masamori and Masuyo were married on August 25, 1918 at the Japanese Baptist Church in Tacoma, Washington.

Masamori Sato was born on December 1, 1885, the third son of Zenzaemon and Tsuru (Nee Ishikawa) Sato of Kata Mura, Kawanabe Gun, Kagoshima prefecture, Island of Kyushu, Japan. Masamori came to this country at the age of 27, stepping ashore at Tacoma on October 12, 1912. For five years he worked in a sawmill near Tacoma; on the railroad near Three Forks, Montana, and Othello, Washington; and on the Yamada farm in Firwood, near Puyallup, Washington before starting his own farm in Firwood.

Masuyo Ishikawa was born on May 19, 1898, the oldest daughter of Takijiro and Matsuno (Nee Fukunaga) Ishikawa of Yasa Mura, Asakura Gun, Fukuoka Prefecture, Island of Kyushu, Japan. Masuyo and her sister had immigrated to this country in April 1916 to join her father and stepmother, and half-sister who were already living and farming in Firwood. Masuyo's family returned to Japan around 1921.

Permanent Return to Japan

At the time when Mr. Ishikawa was returning to Japan, the country was experiencing a very struggling economy. But because Mr. Ishikawa had prospered in America, he was able to afford to take back with him enough Douglas fir tree lumber from Washington to build a house for himself. It became a historical home and landmark in the village for many years. The village folks were very impressed with this unique home not made of a thatched roof, but of Kawala (tile), the only tile roof on a home in this entire village.

With its entire grandiose splendor of the time until around 2000, all the holiday socials were hosted there. Ultimately, it was referred to by the village folks as the "Great American Home." It was built in 1922 and was still looking great in 1984, when I visited family there.

The Ishikawa family owned about 40 acres of land where rice was grown. In the wintertime, when the farm was dormant Grandpa would setup an amphitheater to entertain the village folks and folks from near and far with classic performances; he would make very large posters and post them everywhere to advertise the coming events. Besides these shows, he conducted annual horse racing events. To do this, he would hire a jockey who trained the horse ahead of the events and rode the horse in the competition. Knowing his horse always did well, the village folks were the biggest cheering section. When his horse won it gave rise to the anticipation of a big celebration that would follow, and be paid for from the winning prize money.

He spent the money on the village folks lavishly for the theater and future horse racing events. Many folks came from miles without food at a time when refrigeration did not exist. Mr. Ishikawa would involve the whole family in serving food for the weary travelers. The women in the family detested the times when these events occurred, because they were in charge of cooking huge supplies of mainstay, rice along with pickles, and other condiments made two weeks in advance. It was said that Grandpa Ishikawa had a philosophy that "One must be willing to do any menial work to earn a living and sustain his livelihood." So he was creating work ethics and being charitable to the less fortunate.

CHAPTER 2

Depression Years

Masamori and Masuyo continued to farm the leased property from Herbert Berens until 1933. Early in their marriage after their first child, a daughter was born named Yoneko, when their home burned to the ground. This time Masamori rebuilt a home in the same place, this new home included a Japanese bathroom that was fabulous and like none other American-like bathroom. They raised six children, Yoneko (Betty), Hidemitsu (John), Matsuko (Bessie), Satoshi (Bob), Michiko (Rose), and Saburo (Frank). The American names were taken when each child entered into the Firwood Elementary School because Miss Boyle, the first grade teacher, insisted that every child should have an American name just as well as a Japanese one. The children also attended the Tacoma Japanese Methodist Church, usually traveling by a greyhound bus.

When all of us siblings grew to the age of entering first grade, Masamori instituted and founded the Japanese schoolhouse that all the Japanese children in the area could attend. We could walk through our farm field to attend the American school followed by going to the Japanese school each day. When Yoneko went to first grade, the teacher Miss Boyle gave her the name Betty because of her difficulty pronouncing our Japanese names. Gradually, as the rest of us began school, Betty decided to give the rest of us an American name knowing the inevitability of what would happen.

I was the fifth child of six siblings. On the first day of school, I told the teacher that my name was Frances. The teacher was very aware of the whole situation; because in her two-grade classroom, she already had two girls named Frances, so she asked me if she could call me Rose instead. I didn't know what to say, so I just adopted her suggestion. It is still not on my birth certificate, but it has become a legal name because I have used it for 82 years now.

As I reflect back on those years past, I have always thought that I came from a poor family because as children, we did not receive birthday or Christmas gifts. In later years, I learned that there were families living in homes with dirt floors, without home phones, family sedan automobiles, farm trucks, and abundance of homegrown fruits and vegetables that dad raised on our farm to eat.

Masamori and Masuyo were very diligent hard workers working from daylight to dark. This meant dinners were usually quiet late, I was always the "chosen one." I was chosen to walk to the only gas station and grocery store in Firwood about one mile from home to buy loaves of white Wonderbread for our dinner. I was so hungry that I often ate the middles out of the loaves of bread. Mother was very understanding and would never scold me. Dad would sometimes fly off the handle, but mother was always steadfast with enduring patience.

SATO-ISHIKAWA FAMILY TREE (JAPAN)

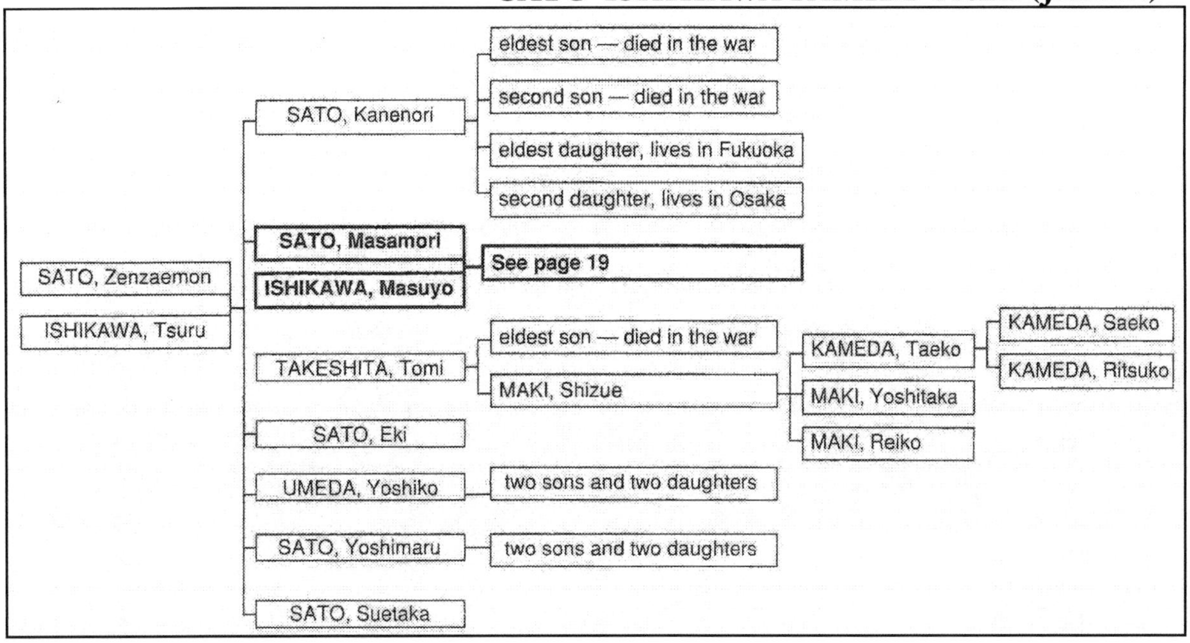

PASSPORTS

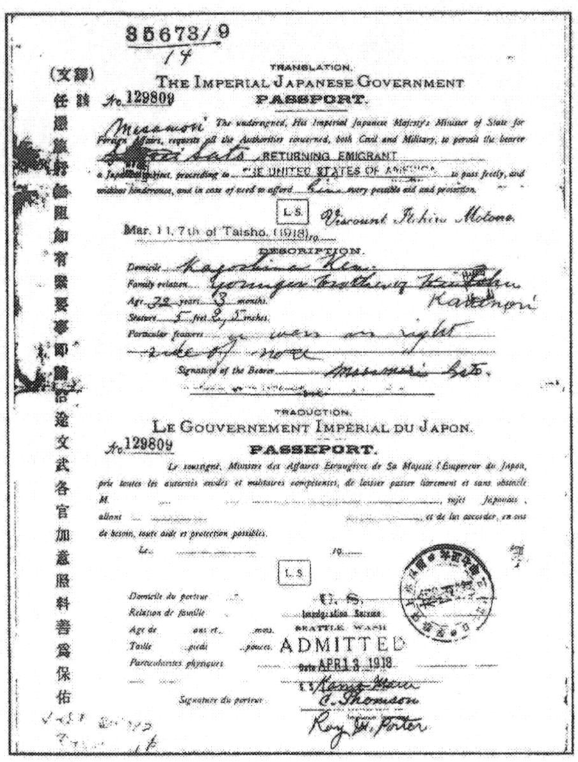

85673/9

(文譯)

TRANSLATION.

THE IMPERIAL JAPANESE GOVERNMENT

No. 129809

PASSPORT.

The undersigned, His Imperial Japanese Majesty's Minister of State for Foreign Affairs, requests all the Authorities concerned, both Civil and Military, to permit the bearer Masamori Sato RETURNING EMIGRANT a Japanese subject, proceeding to THE UNITED STATES OF AMERICA to pass freely, and without hindrance, and in case of need to afford him every possible aid and protection.

L.S. Viscount Ichiro Motono

Mar. 11, 7th of Taisho. (1918)

DESCRIPTION.

Domicile Kagoshima Ken

Family relation Younger brother of Kanenori

Stature 5 feet 2 inches.

Signature of the Bearer Masamori Sato.

TRADUCTION.

LE GOUVERNEMENT IMPÉRIAL DU JAPON.

No. 129809

PASSEPORT.

Le soussigné, Ministre des Affaires Etrangères de Sa Majesté l'Empereur du Japon, prie toutes les autorités civiles et militaires compétentes, de laisser passer librement et sans obstacle M. ..., sujet Japonais, allant ... et de lui accorder, en cas de besoin, toute aide et protection possibles.

Domicile du porteur

Relation de famille

Age de ... ans et ... mois.

Taille ... pieds ... pouces.

Particularités physiques

Signature du porteur.

U. S. Immigration Service SEATTLE, WASH. ADMITTED Date APR 13 1918

C. Thomson

Roy H. Porter

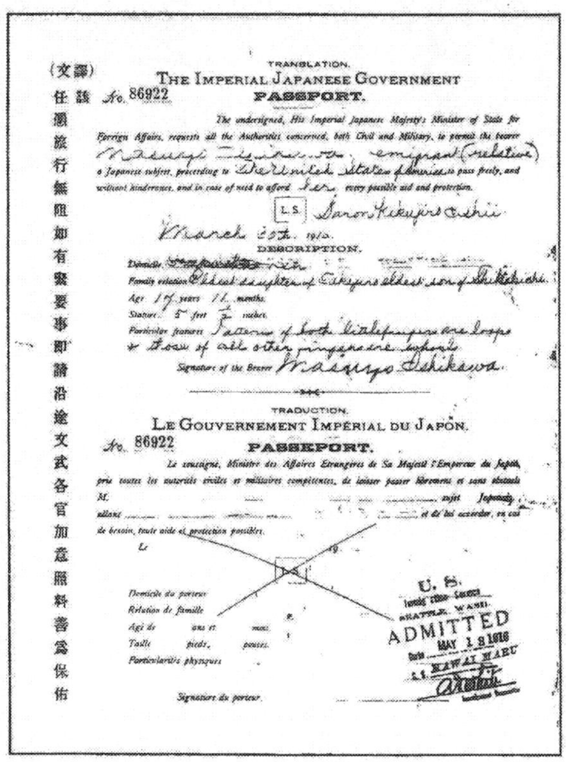

(文譯)

TRANSLATION.

THE IMPERIAL JAPANESE GOVERNMENT

No. 86922

PASSPORT.

The undersigned, His Imperial Japanese Majesty's Minister of State for Foreign Affairs, requests all the Authorities concerned, both Civil and Military, to permit the bearer Masuyo Ishikawa, emigrant (relative) a Japanese subject, proceeding to the United States of America to pass freely, and without hindrance, and in case of need to afford her every possible aid and protection.

L.S. Baron Kikujiro Ishii

March 1918

DESCRIPTION.

Family relation Eldest daughter of Eikujiro eldest son of ...

Age 17 years 11 months.

Stature 5 feet ... inches.

Particular features Pattern of both little fingers are loops & those of all other fingers are whorls

Signature of the Bearer Masuyo Ishikawa.

TRADUCTION.

LE GOUVERNEMENT IMPÉRIAL DU JAPON.

No. 86922

PASSEPORT.

Le soussigné, Ministre des Affaires Etrangères de Sa Majesté l'Empereur du Japon, prie toutes les autorités civiles et militaires compétentes, de laisser passer librement et sans obstacle M. ..., sujet Japonais, allant ... et de lui accorder, en cas de besoin, toute aide et protection possibles.

Domicile du porteur

Relation de famille

Age de ... ans et ... mois.

Taille ... pieds ... pouces.

Particularités physiques

Signature du porteur.

U. S. Immigration Service SEATTLE, WASH. ADMITTED Date MAY 18 1918 S.S. KAWAI MARU

ORIGINAL

No. 716162

Petition No.

Seal

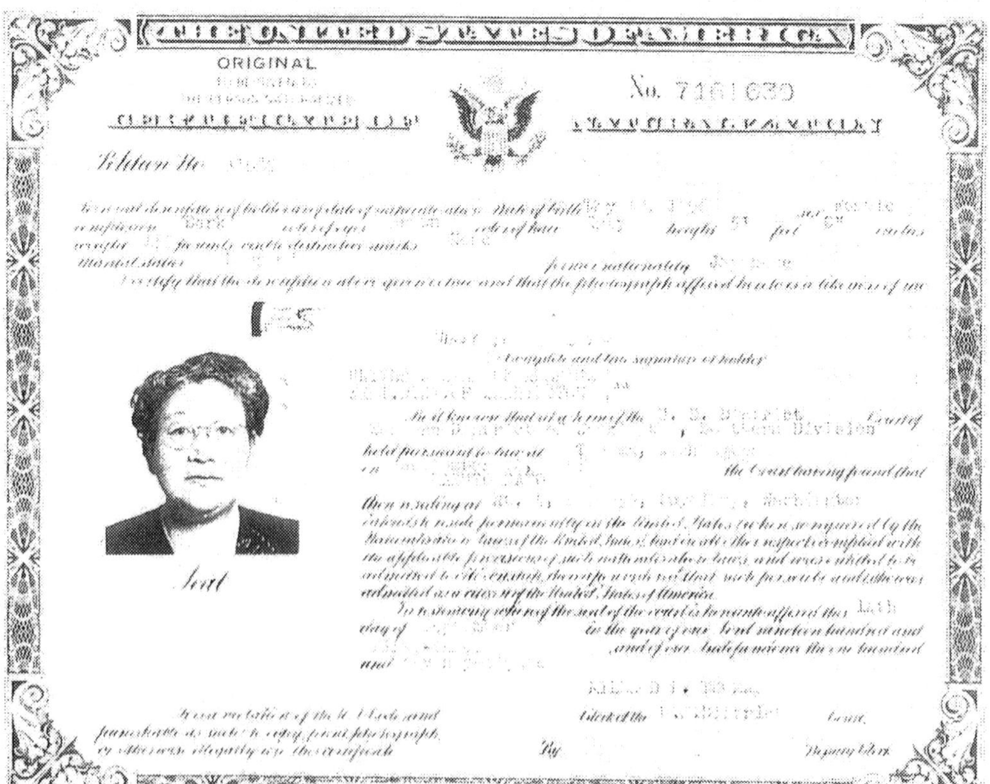
ORIGINAL

No. 7161630

Petition No.

Seal

ISHIKAWA FAMILY IN JAPAN

Back row: Ishiyo, Kinji (Ishiyo's husband), Shizuko.
Front row: Masae, Shigeko, Haruko, Takejiro, Takejiro's second wife (name unknown), Kazuhiro (baby)

SATO FAMILY IN JAPAN

Standing: Suetaka, Masamori, Kanemori, Yoshinari.
Sitting: Tomi Takeshita with son Atashi Takeshita, Yoshi, Tsura, Shizue Takeshita, Eki

Left: (Masuyo's father) Takijiro Sato and stepmother Tsuru

Left: (Masuyo's brother-in-law) Kinji Ishikawa and sister Ishio

MASAMORI SATO

On the Sandberg farm, Firwood, Washington, around 1916.

Masamori as a student, in Japan, before 1912.

Photo taken during last trip to Japan in 1918.

Photo taken during last trip to Japan in 1918.

Masamori Sato and Masuyo Ishikawa were married on August 25, 1918 (registered on August 26) at the Japanese Baptist Church in Tacoma, Washington. Masamori was 32 years old, and Masuyo was 20 years old.

Fall, 1919: trip to Tacoma and an unplanned photo session. "On the spur of the moment, Masamori wanted to get a picture taken, hence his muddy shoes," Betty (Yoneko) was about 4 months old.

Family picture without
Rose and Frank

About 1926, Masamori 41, Masuyo 28
Betty 7, John 5, Bessie 3, Bob 1

PREWAR YEARS

About 1932.
Masamori 46, Masuyo 33, Betty 13, John 11, Bessie 9, Bob 7, Rose 5, Frank 3.

POSTWAR YEARS

1948: Puyallup.
Masamori 62, Masuyo 49, Betty 29, John 27, Bessie 25, Bob 23, Rose 21, Frank 19.

ANNIVERSARY PICTURES

1944, Twin Falls, Idaho.
Year after Silver Aniversary (25th anniversary spent in Minidoka Relocation Camp). Masamori 58, Masuyo 46.

1968, Seattle, Washington
Golden (50th) Aniversary.
Masamori 82, Masuyo 70.

Photo taken in the fall of 1970 in Seattle, Washington. Masamori 85, Masuyo 72.

Chapter 3

Moving to Sumner

The 1930's were the Great Depression years. The dust bowl conditions in the Midwest states aggravated the economic plight of all Americans. The young Sato family managed to make a modest living growing strawberries, raspberries, cucumbers, and broccoli. In 1933, after operating two farms for several years, Masamori moved his family to the Sumner farm where he continued truck farming until 1942.

In 1933, at midterm of my first grade, our family moved seven miles south to a town called Sumner. Dad had leased a farm with a house on the property. We had graduated into a large country farmhouse; I just loved this new home. It had a wrap-around porch on one side of the house that was lined with apple trees on that same side of the house. These trees had lots of juicy banana apples on them that also gave some wonderful cool shade to the porch in the summer.

In the efforts towards the preservation of keeping our Japanese culture alive, Masamori extended his pioneering efforts towards this endeavor. He promoted the setting up of another Japanese school. He put his heart and soul into every facet of the management team as a strong representative of the school board. He thought it was very important to have the best teachers for the children, so he hired them straight from Japan. I didn't like attending the school, but dad made all of us go there after the American school until the ninth grade for five days a week.

The school bus always picked us up in the morning for regular school. But after Japanese school, we were to ride home with Murakami boys who lived further down the highway from us. The three Murakami boys, my two brothers, and I (the only girl) were crammed into the Austin car about the size of a Volkswagen. This meant that I had to sit on somebody's lap so at every chance I could; I would quickly sneak out as fast as I could so the boy's couldn't find me. Then, I would walk the two mile stretch along the highway by myself alone. Talk about child abuse, dad was always infuriated with me and I got real spankings. Often, my brother John would come to my rescue. I was very obstinate, so the spankings didn't stop me from walking home.

At the end of the school year came graduation for all the grades. This was the major event of the school year and recitations, dances, and songs were performed by all the students. Mother was always very busy because she was the only mother who knew how to dress and tie the obi sashes for the kimono's worn at the dances. Because this was an all day event, the mother's would make Japanese potluck food for the dinner. Dad was noted for his beautiful calligraphy. He would always make many huge banners and post them along the walls in his handwriting especially made for those special occasions.

He took a very active part on the school board meetings where Japanese rice wine was served at all of their meetings. When these meetings had ended, he would usually be inebriated and sleepy. In the morning when he finally dragged himself into the house usually about 7 a.m., he always looked a mess. Mother was always relieved to have him home in one piece, so there was never any harsh words spoken.

Creative Farming

In the early spring, he made cold frames for growing vegetable plants that would be set out on the farm, when they became large enough to be transplanted outdoors when the weather warmed up. The cold frames were used over and over for many years until they needed to be repaired. Dad grew celery, lettuce, peas, beans, strawberries, and rhubarb on his farm.

In the fall, when the farm became quiet, he invariably went out searching for better quality seeds and strawberry plants. When he would find a new variety that he liked, he would always come home very excited. This kind of search always paid off because the better quality produce meant a much higher grade rating and profit when he took his produce to the Farmer's Market Association Packing Plant.

When his rhubarb that was grown outdoors in the summer were ready for harvest it always developed a beautiful crimson red color. However, in the fall when the rhubarb roots became dormant, they had to dig up the heavy, huge 2 1/2 foot tubers with a tractor. The tractor then pulled a long sled to haul the tubers to the barn-like shed. This process always included a two-people team to lift these tubers onto the sled into the indoor shed.

He then used a unique technique of twenty-four hour forced indoor growing system for harvesting winter rhubarb. It had regular lights strung to the full length of the shed with coal burning potbelly stoves at each end of the shed for warmth and a sprinkler system for watering indoors. This method developed and brought forth beautiful, sweet-tasting, and pink-colored rhubarb. The different growing methods could make one think that these two-types of rhubarb if seen together at the market were from a different variety of plants, when actually it was merely the two growing methods that made them different. The outdoor rhubarb are vibrant red and quiet tart, while the indoor hothouse rhubarb are pink and milder requiring less sugar for the pallet. Rhubarb sauce was dad's favorite dessert.

After working very long hours on the farm daily his main enjoyment was to read his three Japanese newspapers from Chicago, New York, and Seattle. Because mother's eyes were so poor, she would often sit beside dad after dinner for him to fill her in on all the world and local news; he always read voraciously.

Chapter 4

The Unsettling Years

Because of Masamori's virtuousness for managing his own farm so well, his methods developed even better produce than any of the other farmers who esteemed him of his ingenuity until the bombing of Pearl Harbor in Hawaii, December 7, 1942, when the WWII (World War II) was declared. This meant that all the Japanese on the West Coast of Washington, Oregon, California, Alaska, and Peru, South America were to be incarcerated into eleven camps by the Executive Order 9099 by President Franklin D. Roosevelt. We were given two month's notice of incarceration.

Betty, age twenty-two, who was the oldest of us siblings along with my brother John who was twenty and was put in charge of helping our parents to sell our farm equipment, the vegetables that were already planted on our farm, and all of our household items. It was a very hurry scurry job for them as people were trying to take advantage of the two young folks helping our parents the best they knew how in selling and storing what they thought they should keep. They even sought consultation from a lawyer about how they should handle the situation like this.

When we entered the Washington State Fairgrounds Assembly Center in May 1942 ironically called Camp Harmony, as ordered by the Presidential Executive Order 9099 on February 19, 1942. Some of the families were crowded into bare bones animal stalls, while others were situated into better quarters.

When fall came, we were relocated to Hunt, Idaho to a camp in Minidoka County located in southern Idaho. The government had built ten other internment camps in the western sector of the U.S. Our housing was like Army barrack structures. The course of summer came with dust storms that entered into our poorly sealed windows. We slept on cots with bags of straw for mattresses and a coal burning potbelly stove for warmth during the winter. There was a "mess hall" where the meals were served and public washboard sinks to launder clothes with an open air showering area. Missionary teachers were hired to teach the school children. From within the camp, people could get jobs for $12.00/monthly to $19.00/monthly working as professionals, doctors, dentists, in the administration offices, or at the camp farm. Mother worked in the laundry facility for the hospital.

During the first year of incarceration, the recruitment service came to our camp looking for volunteers for the armed services. It wasn't until at that time that my oldest brother decided to volunteer. He became part of the Intelligence Service and spent his overseas time in Guam and Japan translating Japanese into English. After the first year in camp my brother Bob graduated high school and then he received orders for induction into the service also. Betty was given leave for higher education and went into Nurse's Training in Colorado Springs, Colorado. Bessie went to Rochester, Minnesota, to complete her Nurse's Training that she had started before WWII began.

During camp internment, dad was given leave to go to work on a turkey farm in Wendell, Idaho. Mother joined dad about five months later. This now left my younger brother Frank age 16 and myself age 18 in camp, when the war was declared over. Our family was now scattered all over the world so it seemed from Guam, France, Colorado, Minnesota, Wendell, Idaho, and Minedoka, Idaho.

When the war ended, we were notified of the camp closing. We all began to have a renewed feeling of a brighter future and everyone was released and given the choice to go wherever they chose to go. Frank and I chose to join our sister Bessie in Rochester, Minnesota and to attend school there. Through her influence, she found a place in the home of Dr. Halburg for me. He was an eye, ear, and nose specialists at the Mayo Clinic. Frank went to live with Bessie.

That was where I learned to cook. I did light housework and became an expert nanny for their two sweet children Gretha Ann and red haired Rusty. While I was there, I graduated high school. All the students were very apprehensive of us both because they had never known any Japanese before we came along. But soon after Christmas, they all became our best friends. By this time mother and dad had left their turkey farming jobs and resettled in Twin Falls, Idaho.

Then after my graduation, Frank and I both left Minnesota to join our parents. They were living in a farming settlement with cottages for farm laborers built by the government. It was very simple housing with the basic needs: a kitchen, bathrooms, and bedrooms. John had already returned from the service in Guam and Japan. Frank finished high school in Twin Falls; soon Bob also joined us from the service in France. The farm crew that our parents worked with were all friends from Sumner, Washington. The chosen foreman would get contracts by the acre to harvest the onions and potatoes or to weed the vegetable fields.

June 1945, Hunt Idaho Minidoka War Camp
structures we called home.

Masuyo, Masamori

Rose, Masuyo, Betty, Masamori

Chapter 5

The Family Gathering

In 1948, Masamori and Masuyo decided to return back to Washington. Bessie had already left Rochester, Minnesota while Betty also left Colorado Springs, Colorado to return to Washington. When we all returned to Washington it reminded me about the gathering of Israel story in the Bible. I'm sure dad was envisioning the full meaning of his American dream!

I was planning to go along with my parents and my brothers John, Bob, and Frank when a gentleman came looking for someone to help his wife in their home in Meridian, Idaho. It turned out that he was the President of the Veterinarian Association of Idaho. Dr. Rene Derrer was a practicing veterinarian in Boise, Idaho. I agreed to accept the job because his wife needed help from her recent health complications. I became a "gopher." I helped his wife cook family meals, learned to cook, clean house, helped to hold down the animals when the doctor performed surgery, and ran errands to town. On my days off on Sunday's, I would take their four year old son Steven on the Greyhound bus to go to see movies like Bambi in Boise.

At home there, I usually dressed in baggy sweaters and jeans. However, on these outings, I would wear a dress and high heels although I was only 19 years old. Steven was always impressed with my attire and commented, "Rose, you look like a lady!" This remark made me feel very grown up. My position only lasted four months, but we became good friends. They thought so much of me that they even came to visit me in Washington. For years, they corresponded with me until they both passed away.

After leaving work with Dr. Rene Derrer, a veterinarian; I then join my parents in Washington, I learned dad and mother had settled on a small country mini farm in Puyallup, Washington. Betty and Bessie located to Seattle, Washington and were already employed as Registered Nurses.

John and Bob were attending the University of Washington. Then, Frank also began at the University of Washington; and I enrolled in Charette School of Costume and Design in Seattle. While all of us kids went off to Seattle, Masamori and Masuyo raised raspberries and fabulous sweet Freestone Hale peaches on their mini farm.

August 22, 1965. Whitney Church, Tacoma.
Back row: Martin Brinitzer, Jennifer Stults, Hugh Stults, Minoru Okura.
Second row: Frank Sato, Dean Sato, June Sato, Ann Brinitzer, Marc Brinitzer, Bessie Brinitzer, Matthew Brinitzer, Rose Stults, Betty Okura, Brian Okura, James Okura, Ruth Sato, John Sato, Aster Sato, Bob Sato, Samuel Sato.
Front row: Gregory Sato, Teresa Sato, Glen Sato, John R. Sato, Craig Brinitzer, Masuyo Sato, Andy Stults, Masamori Sato, Arthur Sato, Amy Sato, Kent Sato, Stanley Sato, Joan Sato, Richard Sato.

The Super Farmer

One day while mother and dad were working on their beautiful yard, a young farmer by the name of George Rickter who lived just down their street remembered dad from the pre-war Farmer's Market days. When he went home and mentioned it to his wife, she insisted that he should go back to see if this man was the same Mr. Sato that he remembered at that time at the Farmer's Market with his exceptional produce everyone admired. George was a very young man about the age of 18 years old before WWII. He was living with his parents and taking their produce to the Farmer's Market for them. Now eight years or later, he had inherited the family homestead and was truck farming the land.

Dad was probably about the age of 64, when George came to see him and mother. He learned dad was the same Mr. Sato from the pre-war years at the Farmer's Market. Dad said he was too old to do work worth any payment from George, but George said he didn't care about that because the real reason he wanted them to work for him was "mostly for their expert advice." In going to work for George, they had their own unique methods of growing and packing all the produce into crates, which increased the appearance rating at the Farmer's Packing Plant for a greater profit.

Through the years that mother and dad went to work for George, he was so grateful for all their help that he always rewarded them lavishly at Christmas. He insisted on paying his part towards social security, so they could receive social security benefits. After the many years of success, George's son Ed succeeded him, dad was grateful for that blessing.

It was around that time, when Betty's husband died leaving only she and two very young and growing boys. Then soon after retirement, Masuyo had had a heart attack, so Betty was traveling making frequent sixty-five mile roundtrips between Seattle and Puyallup to look in on the folks that needed some medical assistance. She was checking their health and giving shots when needed as a registered nurse.

Betty had a modest size home in Seattle. It was not adequate for mother, dad, and her two boys, and because the folks were showing deteriorating signs of their years; they both decided that they should sell their homes and buy a larger replacement home that would accommodate all five of them in Seattle. A few years later, mother's heart worsened, and she died of a heart attack. Dad's general health gradually deteriorated, so he went to live in a Japanese-managed nursing home. He was the first resident to be admitted there. In his late life, he became rather quiet amiable enjoying the attention of the staff. He became very special to all of the staff who loved him dearly. When I visited the family in Seattle on vacation, I would visit dad at lunch time with his favorite hamburger, French-fries, and milkshake; his eyes would always light up with delight. While residing at the nursing home he died in the dining room while eating pineapple that had gotten lodged in his throat. When he died at the age of 92, he had lived a long, happy, fulfilled life in America.

The influences that Masamori and Masuyo made to all of their bright upstanding and accomplished children are listed from the oldest to the youngest are: Yoneko (Betty), Hidemitsu (John), Matsuko (Bessie), Satoshi (Bob), Michiko (Rose), and Saburo (Frank).

Chapter 6

Sons and Daughters

Betty

Rose's recollections of her sister Betty are as follows because Betty became the matriarch of the family at an early age as she became very astute to the American customs and legal matters. Much of this became important to our parents who couldn't speak or understand the laws of the land. Betty was able to fulfill all their needs with help through inquiry and interpreting for them at a legal dog bite case. She helped dad with negotiations at the Farmer's Associations.

She also helped to institute the development of the J.A.C.L. organization (Japanese American Citizens League). This organization was for the benefit of all the parents who were not able to handle their legal problems, and it helped to alleviate the language barriers of the senior Japanese on the West Coast. This organization was a prewar endeavor on the West Coast before WWII and eventually became a national organization after WWII.

In the winter time when the farm became inactive, she went to work at a dentist's home doing household duties such as cooking and cleaning. This was how she learned many American customs; she also befriended older women who taught her many additional skills including etiquette. These experiences enriched all of our lives. When about the age of 19 or so, she was canning a thousand jars of various fruits and vegetables for our family. I loved helping her; she was proud of herself and knew how proudly dad depended on her because she even managed the family finances. The leased farm came with a gasoline pump; this was why dad had gasoline delivered to the farm to be used on the farm. When Betty learned that by keeping good records of these deliveries, she could receive rewards by the amount that was delivered. In this way, she was able to get a twelve setting China set for our family the first time, and then the family silverware the second time.

During the early incarceration, she left the camp to attend the Seton School of Nursing at Colorado Springs, Colorado. By the end of WWII as mentioned before, we all returned back to Washington. But as a surgical nurse at the Harborview Hospital in Seattle, she helped develop the 911 medical service which became the basis on the television program that was featured for several years and it also became the national emergency number. But as a training nurse at the hospital, she often spent hours at the local library on her off hours searching and making visual aids for her students.

During her first marriage to Min Okura, she had two sons named Brian and Jimmy. After Min's passing, she remarried Yo Maekawa who also has passed away now. She continues to live in Seattle, now at the age of 88; she has a beautiful vegetable and flower garden and is quiet active with her church family.

Exhibit A
Edited Transcript

To: Commission on Wartime Relocation and Internment of Citizens
From: Betty Y. Okura
Date: July 31, 1981
Re: Pre-evacuation, camp life and resettlement following internment

Madame Chairperson and members of the commission:

I am Betty Okura, a registered nurse, having received a license to practice in the state of Colorado in 1946 and in the state of Washington in 1947. But as of April 1, 1980, I have retired from nursing at the Harborview Medical Center, Operating Room Department. I am the age of 62 years old.

So that our children, grandchildren, and generations to come, and also other ethnic groups which may not be subjected to the kinds of experiences that we encountered following the bombing of Pearl Harbor by the Japanese on December 7, 1941 and subsequent declaration of war against Japan. I have to share with you these experiences as they happened to me and other members of my family.

The aftermath of Pearl Harbor

We were a family of eight, farming in Sumner, Washington. In 1941, father was 56 years old and mother was 43. I was the oldest, at age 22, and John was 20 and was a junior at the University of Washington in Seattle. Bessie age 18; was a first-year nursing student in Tacoma, Washington. Robert age 16; was a junior in high school. Rose age 14; was in the ninth grade and Frank age 12; was in the seventh grade. December 7, 1941 started out as any other farming day for that time of year. We planted Rockhill everbearing strawberries all day so we were not aware of the day's events until that evening. What a terrible feeling that was, to hear the news! Suddenly, the happiness and security of our home was gone.

Each of the following days, we heard of some Issei father was being taken away by the FBI and wondered on what charges he was being held. Was it justifiable? Our father informed us that since he was an alien (i.e., not an American citizen, as U.S. law forbade Asians to become naturalized) he might also be taken, though he was not aware of having done any wrong. We all believed that we American-born citizen children would not be taken; for our father had always told us that we had picked the best country in the world to live in. Still, our hearts were heavy, wondering what was to become of us. We kept our feelings to ourselves as we shed our tears alone and I asked God to help us understand, to keep us together, and to guide us. John came home from college at the end of the winter quarter. Bessie was to have her education interrupted later in the spring. The younger three came home from school each day with unhappiness and worry written all over their faces. We were to leave Sumner less than a month before the school year ended, on May 14, 1942.

Preparation for Evacuation

Everyday after the bombing of Pearl Harbor, events began to point toward evacuation of the Japanese from the West Coast. In my belief that my country would not evacuate us, I mentally started to formulate plans so John and I could manage the farm and keep the family together, should our parents be taken away. How naïve I was!

On February 19, 1942, an Executive Order 9099 was issued. That order authorized the Army to designate military zones from which all and any persons could be excluded; that meant evacuation of American citizens of the Japanese ancestry (the Nisei and Sansei) as well as the Japanese nationals (the Issei). For me, that was a day never to be forgotten, one of utter despair and feelings of being unwanted by my country. Though we were American citizens, we had the wrong color of skin, hair, and eyes. How could this country, my country, do this to me? This was the only country I knew. If it had not been for our neighbors, the Kilborns, at that point in my life I don't think I could have weathered the following days.

Slowly, the idealist in me turned to reality and preparations for evacuations had begun. During all this time, December through spring, farming went on. Father thought this would be best. But his logic was that produce would be needed, whether or not we would be there to harvest it. In retrospect, it was helpful for us since it kept us very bus and occupied for a great part of the day. So, with heavy hearts, the crops were planted, and life went on.

But to prepare for the evacuation, our assets on the farm would have to be liquidated if we were to have any funds to reestablish ourselves after the crisis was over. Our farm land was leased, but a considerable sun had been invested in building two large rhubarb houses, converting a cattle shed, and building a large greenhouse and cold frames. In addition to these assets, we had the usual equipment used in operating a farm, plus supplies. Together with my folks, John and I did an inventory and arrived at a price for selling our assets.

A young man who had previously worked for us came to buy our assets and to take over the farm. However, he would not even consider father's price. He told us very bluntly that we had to sell at this price, since we would have to leave anyway. You can imagine how upset we were. For our father, this was especially a very distressing time. The young man had worked for us for several years after he first arrived from the Philippines. Our father had shown him many details regarding farm work. Father became very depressed, with the increasing problems of the evacuation. It was so much that he seriously considered just abandoning everything instead of giving into the young man.

I can remember how upset I was. The injustice of the whole thing, but for the first time in my life, I didn't sleep that night, because of my anger. We couldn't let our parents throw away their lifetime assets on the farm! There had to be something that we could be done. So, John and I went to see the Farm Security Agency office in Tacoma, and received the necessary information and forms. We filled out the forms, describing our farm with its crops, equipment, and supplies. After filing with the FSA, we were matched with a family looking for a farm, and a sale was made. We received a check before going to the War Relocation Camp. John wrote earlier this year, March 1, 1981: "All I remember is that we thought we got so very little, but I don't remember the amounts." (Records from the filing have been destroyed and are not available for proof.)

The Puyallup J.A.C.L. during that time provided support and help for many families needing assistance with the evacuation. Since a curfew was in force, all activities had to be done within the hours allowed. When we left Sumner, a few pieces of furniture such as beds, a chest of drawers, one daveno, a chair, and some kitchen utensils were stored in the attic of our landlord's home. The space was a limited factor; and we could not store all of our possessions. The remaining furnishings of our home were left with the new family for a small sum. They were from the Midwest, escaping that dust-stricken area for the lush Pacific Northwest, and they had six small children.

Our business matters were taken care of, and father assigned Power of Attorney to Mr. Gregory with the First National Bank in Puyallup. Father had done business with him for many years.

The Puyallup Assembly Center

On May 14, 1942, we arrived at the Puyallup Assembly Center, which was called "Camp Harmony," with our baggage, which was one piece of luggage and bedding for each person. I remember father loading all of us in the back of the truck, and driving the five miles south of Sumner. It was a grim trip, all of us wondering if we would ever see our valley again. For some reason, I drove the truck back to Sumner and was brought back by one of our neighbors.

While at the Puyallup Assembly Center, we were assigned to Area B. Our living space was one room for the seven of us. Bessie was in the nurse's quarters in the hospital area, Area D. Our single beds were army cots with straw-filled mattresses, which were lined up next to each other with very little space in between. We did not get to see Bessie very often, since going from one area to another which was not easily done.

It was very difficult to adjust to because of the loss of privacy. The toilets and bathing facilities were all community-style, and we ate in the mess halls. Children began to have their meals with their friends and no longer with their parents. These conditions resulted in the failing part of parental authority and family life in general. It was even harder to adjust to the being behind fences with barbed wire and with soldiers standing in the high watchtowers. Many not much older than me, I wondered if they ever gave us a thought. We were Americans just like them, but placed in these concentration camps with no trial, no convictions just the wrong ethnic background. Did they think this was justifiable? If it had not been for the friends who came to the gate to see us in Puyallup, our days would have been much more depressing. We also tried to support each other in our problems and adjusting to difficult conditions.

The Minidoka War Relocation Camp

In the fall of 1942, we were moved to the Minidoka War Relocation Camp, near Twin Falls, Idaho I think they found the dirtiest and oldest train in the country for us. After the long ride, we found ourselves in the middle of southern Idaho, on a railroad siding, in the midst of a sagebrush desert. From there we were transported to the camp.

When we arrived at Minidoka, we were assigned to Block #19, the seven of us was once again in one room. This time the room was somewhat larger than in Puyallup, but still inadequate for seven grown people. There was no vegetation in the newly-constructed areas, and the sand storms were furious. Sand sifted into the rooms everywhere, through cracks in the walls, from the sills and jambs of the poorly-constructed windows and doors. But at times we had to place dampened handkerchiefs or towels over our noses and mouths so we could breathe. People with allergies and asthma were in great discomfort.

That winter the weather was extremely severe compared to what we were accustomed to in the Northwest. It was bitterly cold and windy, which added much tribulation for the camp population. That winter there were so many illnesses due to the change in the environment and because of the location of the mess halls, laundry, bathing, and toilet facilities; this meant having to bare the elements several times daily. There was a flu epidemic that winter; the children and the elderly seemed to be the most susceptible. The Pediatric ward #10 was always full of little ones with diarrhea and consequent problems. But because of the cold weather, the elderly that had circulatory problems had more than their share of troubles too. The faculty plumbing had hastily-constructed the hospital which made conditions worse.

Shortly after I arrived in Minidoka, I applied for a nurse's aide position and was accepted. But after a series of orientation training sessions, we were then placed in the hospital wards. I believe that the pay was $12/monthly for unskilled, $16/monthly for skilled, and $19/monthly for professionals. I started at $12/monthly and received a raise to $16/monthly before leaving the camp. The hospital was 19 blocks from our barrack room. But as the fall weather turned into winter, it became increasingly difficult to get to and from work. Finally an ambulance pick-up for the hospital staff was instituted. Eventually, I moved into a room next to the hospital area, which helped slightly to relieve the congestion in our family's one-room barrack.

But early in the spring of 1943, I started writing to various nursing schools for admittance into their programs; and I received many negative responses. They ranged from "We would like to consider you, however, due to the communities feelings; it is not advisable to admit you at this time..." to "We are not accepting anyone of the Japanese ancestry." Finally, I was accepted by the Sisters of Charity,

Glockner-Penrose Hospital in Colorado Springs, Colorado. The classes at Seton School of Nursing began on July 1, 1943, and I left Minidoka War Relocation Camp on June 26, 1943.

The Resettlement

My brother John started working as a warehouseman shortly after arriving in Minidoka, and he continued to work until the following spring, which at the time he volunteered for the Army. He left Minidoka in the last part of May of 1943, and was eventually to go overseas in the Pacific and was assigned to the Air Force Intelligence Division. My sister Bessie also had some difficulty in getting accepted into a nursing school. She left during the first winter for St. Mary's Hospital in Rochester, Minnesota. While she was in the camp, she worked as student nurse. To this day, I still have a soft spot in my heart for the Catholic sisters who took us into nursing when others were afraid to do so.

Bob had finished his last year of high school with the first graduating senior class at Hunt High School in Minidoka. But shortly after graduating in July of 1943, he was drafted into the Army in May and joined the 442nd Regiment in Europe in October of 1944. Rose and Frank were coping with camp life, and was attending the makeshift camp school and wondering what was to become of them. For the first time in their lives, the family was no longer together, but was scattered throughout the country.

Mother had begun to work in the hospital laundry and found it to require some adjustments, since she had previously worked only in farming. Father had some health problems and was hospitalized for only a short time. But after some months of inactivity, he worked as an ambulance driver. In 1944, father left Minidoka to work on a turkey ranch just outside of Minidoka in Wendell, Idaho. But because of the lack of housing accommodations, he went alone. He felt very strongly that it was important to get out and get started again.

It was very hard for everyone to bear these developments in their lives. In addition, we all knew that John and Bob would soon be going overseas. This was particularly stressful for mother and father. This was an educational picture for the youngest members of the family, but Rose and Frank posed another problem as the schools in Minidoka were closing. It was decided that they should go live with my sister Bessie in Rochester, Minnesota, since she had already finished her nurse's training. So once again, Rose and Frank were uprooted to a strange community. Frank lived with Bessie, and Rose who by then was in her senior year, worked as a schoolgirl in a home. For the fifteen year old and the seventeen year old children, who had spent their last several years in isolated areas, this was a frightening experience.

Shortly after Rose and Frank left for Minnesota, mother was able to get employment from father's employer and soon she joined him in Wendell. She also took care of the turkeys, a flock being about 4,000-7,000 birds. They worked within sight of each other, but they had to walk quiet a way to meet and eat dinner together. It's a wonder they didn't meet a rattlesnake unexpectedly, for the area was teeming with them. They each lived in a very small trailer house under extremely primitive conditions.

After the end of the 1945-46 school year; Rose and Frank joined their mother and father in Twin Falls, where Frank finished his last year of high school. The family worked in the fields and in warehouses while making plans to return home to the Pacific Northwest. In 1948, mother and father purchased a home in Puyallup on one acre, which provided income for them. They also worked for several years on the Richter farm to supplement their income. But by that time, all the family was back in the Pacific Northwest area. Some of us had finished our education, while others were still in school.

In spite of all the heartaches, injustices, discriminations, and hardships of the years past; we were finally able to look ahead and plan for the future.

End of "Exhibit A" Transcript

John

John was the Ichibon (#1) son of Masamori. But because dad resented the privileged position of the caste system, I felt that dad never realized or saw John's brilliance or potential. I thought John was not always treated fairly. From about the age of 15, he was expected to do a man's job by driving the farm equipment and the family vehicle for chauffeuring all of his siblings. It enriched the social life for the rest of us kids in the family, and we were able to go on family picnics, to the annual daffodil parades, to the local country store for firecrackers on the 4th of July. He was so smart that he often stumped the physics teacher with physics problems that he made up.

While incarcerated in Hunt, Idaho camp, recruitment officers came into our camp seeking volunteers to be inducted into the armed services. John volunteered in 1943 to join the 442nd Regimental Combat Team which was being assembled at Camp Shelby in Mississippi. He was assigned to the 522nd Field Artillery Battalion, but because of the urgent need for Japanese linguists, the Army transferred him to the Military Intelligence Service, where he served with the 20th Air Force on Tinian Island, South Pacific. An interesting sidelight: he chanced to meet his former Japanese school teacher, Miss Hiroko Iwanaga, in Tokyo during a mission to gather scientific information shortly after the dropping of the second atomic bomb. John returned to the United States in February of 1946. He then helped his parents move from the turkey farm in Wendell, Idaho to a farm labor camp in Twin Falls.

The following year as Frank and Rose joined them from Minnesota along with Bob's return from fighting in France and Italy, we all returned to Washington State. With one year left to finish college, John resumed attending the University of Washington. He fraternized with many young men from Hawaii. In August of 1948, he graduated with a business degree and became the first Nisei CPA in the state of Washington. Though he did well and graduated with flying colors, he could not find employment locally in Washington State due to so much discrimination. However, he was able to find employment in Hawaii.

After settling there, he decided to look up one of his U.W. friends by the name of George Ito. In meeting George's family, he was introduced to his sister Ruth. From then on he forgot all of the other relationships that he had had before. They were married and have three children: Amy, Arthur, and Kent.

In 1955-56, I had gone to Hawaii on a vacation. However, when I arrived I found a job working for "Carol and Mary's" Hawaiian dress shop; I stayed in Hawaii for one year. During that time, Ruth informed me about a special invitation that she and John had received to be accepted into the most elite social society in Honolulu, Hawaii. It was an honor and the highlight of John's career as he continued to climb the corporate ladder with American Factors Corporation. He became Chief Financial Officer, Vice President, and Controller for AMFAC and later with General Electric Finance Corporation as Vice President. Today at the age of 86, he lives with his wife Ruth in Oahu, Hawaii and enjoys babysitting his grandchildren.

Bessie

As a child, Bessie could not and would not hold back her emotions as she grew older; she had become quiet meticulous in her ways. We lived in an ordinary farmhouse that lacked the standards of many homes of today. Mother cooked for the eight o us on a wood-burning stove. She would always be very busy cooking at mealtime in the formative years.

One time as mother was busy preparing and serving the meals to us, she overlooked Bessie. She just sat there at the table and said nothing, while everyone else was eating. Bessie's feelings was so hurt, she began sniffling. When mother asked her what was wrong, Bessie wanted to know why she wasn't served dinner. But of course, mother was sorry for the oversight and immediately served her. On the farm, we had a wringer type washing machine and washed about every three to four weeks. Bessie would wash her "undies" by hand and dry them on the cooled down oven rack to dry overnight.

She was still in high school, when she was inspired to become a doctor. However, the family shattered her dreams with discouragement, so she settled on becoming a nurse. She had already completed one year of training before the WWII began. We were all incarcerated to a temporary location at first; then we were given multiple vaccination shots. So anyone with any medical abilities had to help in this endeavor. But because of this, Bessie was separated from the family quarters to the medical compound to be a part of the vaccinating team.

After our transition to the more permanent camp from Washington, to the Minidoka War Relocation Camp in Southern Idaho. Bessie continued to live in the hospital's staff quarters with the $12.00 per month salary. When the time came that one could be allowed to leave the camp in order to pursue a higher education, Bessie decided to finish her nurse's training by attending St. Mary's School of Nursing in Rochester, Minnesota. She graduated in 1945.

When the war was declared over and with the closure of the camp an announcement was made, the two youngest of her siblings were Frank and I; we then left the camp to join Bessie and to attend school there. But after one year of staying there, I graduated high school and Frank and I left to join our parents. Frank finished high school in Twin Falls, Idaho. John and Bob had also joined them in Idaho. From there mother, dad, John, Bob, Frank, and I all returned back to Washington; while Bessie and Betty were also returning to Washington. We were becoming a family again though not under the same roof.

Bessie returned to Seattle in the early of 1947 to work in the Surgery Department at Harborview Hospital, and later for a private physician, Dr. Walter Scott Brown. She married Martin Brinitzer, who worked for Standard Oil/Chevron, and they traveled to San Francisco, Los Angeles, Guatemala, Honduras, Puerto Rico, and San Diego. After we all moved back to Washington, mom and dad bought a home in Puyallup, but all of us siblings moved to attend school or to find employment in nursing in Seattle.

One day Bessie was invited to a hospital staff party given by the interns and nurses at the hospital where she worked. She was excited about meeting someone by the name of Martin but couldn't remember his last name. I had a boyfriend who had a friend by the name of Martin also. The more Bessie would talk about Martin to me; I felt she was describing the Martin I knew. So my friend Jamie and I invited Martin three times to go visit Bessie, but he always chickened out. So then I decided to let him know that I was going to ask him only one more time. Then, what do you know, he decided to go, and this time it was incredible! He turned out to be the same Martin with the last name Brinitzer. He was employed by Standard Oil of California. When they were married, I designed and made Bessie's wedding gown. Bessie has worked as a nurse her entire working years. At the age of 84, she resides in Aldorado Hills, California, with her husband Martin near their son Matthew and has a daughter named Ann and two other sons named Marc and Craig.

Bob

In his youth Bob was a very serious young man. He always did well in school. So, when I failed 4th grade he felt motivated to help me because our parents couldn't read, write, or have command of the English language and was unable to help me. But, I detested his determination and strong will. He always seemed to know his life's direction. In fact all my sisters and brothers seemed to have the same strength of will that I felt that I lacked.

But as the 4th child and being the second son, it seemed to me that he was treated better than his older brother John. He was never scolded and could do no wrong. He finished his last year of high school in Minidoka Hunt Idaho Camp in 1943.

He was drafted out of the internment camp and was sent to Camp Shelby, Mississippi Army Base with the 171st Infantry Battalion. The camp was specifically built and developed for the Japanese Nisei (the 2nd generation of the Japanese) boys. The boys there, with the highest IQ were then sent to Camp Savage, Minnesota. This was a Japanese Intelligence Language School that his older brother John was sent to for a very highly accelerated training of learning 50 Japanese words per week.

Bob remained at the Camp Shelby Army Base and was sent as a replacement, he joined the Charlie Company of the 100th Infantry Battalion and the 442nd Regimental Combat Team in October of 1944, just after the regiment's rescue of the "Lost Battalion" in the Vogues Mountains of France. They became known as the "Go For Broke" regiment.

But much of the training they went through involved obstacles that were made difficult because of their small and short of stature when they had to climb makeshift walls etc… These obstacles were much easier for the taller men. Many times, they were forced to use their ingenuity to overcome their shortcomings. The officers were simply amazed at their skills. Their unique perseverance paid off when they encountered treacherous mountainous maneuvers and faced with their hardest challenges in the European Front.

When the boys had completed their strenuous training, they were sent to Italy and France to fight against Hitler's Army. They were able to overcome their enemies strategies. From childhood, we developed Japanese colloquialism expressions which were to benefit in transmitting secret messages through the airwaves. This outfoxed the enemy in all fronts involving the Japanese boys.

In the mean time during Bob's involvement, they had to help rescue the "Lost Battalion" from Central Texas that were trapped and surrounded by high mountains and heavy German artillery. The generals were baffled as to how they might rescue them. Then, they decided to send 4000 of the 442nd Battalion Japanese boys in there. Out of the 4000 total, there were around 2000 that came out unscathed. This rescue effort has been recorded in a book called "Honor by Fire" by Lynn Crost. She was a war correspondent who covered the Japanese American Nisei for the whole duration of their European Campaign.

When the ending of the war was eminent, the Nisei boys encountered a Jewish prison camp that Hitler's guards had abandoned. The prisoners were just skin and bones and were left without food and water. The boys gave everything they could give them like K-ration, cigarettes, candy, etc….and gave them all they had. When the war was declared over and the boys were sent home to America, they had become the most decorated group of men ever to have a celebration on the White House grounds with food and many of the famous bands to play welcoming music for them for one week.

He then joined his parents in Twin Falls, Idaho. But after working several months as a farm laborer with his parents, he then moved to Chicago in the fall of 1947. He entered the University of Illinois under the G.I. Bill and was transferring one year later to the University of Washington. He graduated as a Civil Engineer in 1951. But after 15 months with the Star Iron and Steel Company in Tacoma, he then worked for the Corps of Engineers building dams and served there for 27 years. But among the many Northwest projects in which he was involved in were: the advanced planning, design and construction of the Hudson Dam and Reservoir, Green River, Washington; Libby Dam and Reservoir, Kootenai River, Montana; Chief Joseph Additional Units, Columbia River, Washington; and Cedar Falls Dam Improvement, Cedar River, Washington.

He was married to a girl from Hawaii named Aster Saito. She died of Leukemia. They had one daughter named Joan and four sons named: Stanley, Richard, Sam, and Mike. Later, he remarried Aster's best friend Lucy who had two sons named: David, and Dean. Today at the age of 82, he lives with his wife Lucy in Seattle. He has had a stroke sometime back, but though he is somewhat handicapped, his strong will keeps him traveling to a variety of places each year. He has continued to improve his stroke condition and has less reliance on his walker. He lives comfortably with his wife Lucy and is close to his church and has friends who live in the same condo complex. Three of his seven children live in the Seattle area while Stanley lives in Hawaii, Dean lives in California, Joan is in Chicago, and Sam is in Kansas (?). But with all of the children scattered around the United States, Bob keeps busy visiting them all as much as possible.

Rose

As a child I was very quiet and shy. We all attended dad's Japanese school (Referred to as "Tip School"). While in the 1st grade, as I walked home from the American school to Tip school, two sisters were always picking on me by hitting, punching, and calling me names. I got so upset that one day, I went straight home through our farm field that came right up the road where both schools were located. When my mother saw me, she just took me by the hand and talked me into going right back. Another time, still the age of 6 in 1933, when everyone in the family were all gone leaving myself, mother, and Sikum the Phillippino farmhand at home, our telephone rang. We had the only phone in our area, so we often received calls that needed to be relayed to the neighbors. But this particular day, mother asked me to stay with Sikum. When she left to relay the message, I suddenly became fearful and distrustful of Sikum because I had never been left at home with anyone outside our family before. I was so relieved to see her, when she finally returned home after an hour.

When I was halfway into the 1st grade, our family moved from Firwood to Sumner, Washington about seven miles south. It was another heavily populated Japanese farm community. I remembered thinking how smart I was while reading all my class assignment at my new school. But little did I realize that I was getting repeated reading lessons. That became my conclusion years later as I went on into the upper grades and ended up failing 4th grade. Reading has always been a struggling factor in my learning process.

Much of W.W.II and the years from 1941 to 1955 were accounts that were already given by my older siblings and their accounts. In 1955, I flew to visit my brother John in Hawaii which ended up to being a one-year extended vacation. While there, I met Janet Goto through John's wife Ruth. Janet was always coaxing me to go on a double date with she, and her boyfriend Jack Barnhill, and his friend Hugh Stults from Texas.

Hugh was in the Army and was stationed at Schoenfield Army Base. We dated until he was going home to be discharged from his two-year service in June of 1956. I didn't know whether anything serious could develop and decided to leave the island at that time also.

But upon returning to Washington, I became employed at the J.C. Penny Company. I was missing Hugh so much that on Labor Day weekend, I flew to see him. We ended up looking for engagement rings. In January 19, 1957; we were married at the Methodist Church in Seattle, Washington. I moved to Texas City,

Texas, where Hugh worked for Amoco Oil Company as a graduate engineer of Texas Tech College.

In the year of 1959, we were transferred to Portland, Maine with the Amoco Oil Company. I was so bored living in the country with no one to interact with, so I went to work with First National Bank of Portland as a bank teller. I did so well at the bank that when Hugh was being transferred to Pittsburgh, Pennsylvania, and that we would be moving, the Bank's President came to tell me that "their loss was going to be someone else's gain." That really uplifted my confidence, because I had never done well at math in school.

Just after our move to Pittsburgh, we registered for adopting a baby. Soon afterwards, we drove south to visit Hugh's parents for Christmas. We were gone for two weeks to Texas. But as soon as we returned home the phone was ringing off the hook. The adoption agency had been calling us the entire time to give us the good new! They told us they had a 9-month old boy available for us. It was a real challenge for us to turn around and try to go south through the snow and with very icy road conditions of Pennsylvania to Florida.

When we reached Miami, we learned that he had been cared for by very loving foster parents. They had even told us that because he had not been released for adoption since infancy and they thought that no one cared to adopt him. So, they decided to apply for this adoption, though no avail to them. We learned that because Andy was Eurasian (of European-Asia background) the agency was hoping for someone of his background that would be seeking to adopt.

We were actually seeking such a child. So when we applied for the adoption, Andy was 9 months old, and the agency knew the wait was worthwhile because we were a perfect fit! It all came about through the grapevine of all the adoption agencies in America.

Andy also seemed to display a connection towards us when we first met him. The foster parents said Andy always displayed a very guarded distance towards everyone except the family of the foster parents. But for us, he was always trying to get our attention. When it came time for his naptime, we would leave for lunch and return again in the afternoon. But, Andy always cried when he saw us leaving. After three days of visiting with Andy, we were allowed to take Andy back home with us to Pittsburgh, Pennsylvania. We named him Andy Gene Stults. Not long after we brought him home, I named him "Curious George" named after the little stuffed monkey with the same curious mind. By the age of 1, Andy was able to tie a bow under the hood of his winter jacket; he could tie his shoelaces, and he was taking apart our wind-up alarm clocks, and he would take apart all of the other toys. He always showed a very creative and inventive ability.

By the time Andy was one and a half years old, we registered again for an adoption so Andy could have a sister or brother. It wasn't long until we learned that a 1 month-old Eurasian baby girl was available for us. Hugh, Andy, and I visited her on Sundays; while only Andy and I went on Wednesdays while Hugh was at work.

But after three months of our twice weekly visits, we were allowed to take her home; and we named her Jennifer Lynn Stults. Andy was very excited because he wished so much for a playmate. While, he waited for her to become his playmate, he would run upstairs to get her clean diapers for me. Then, when it was her naptime; he was willing to put all of her toys into her playpen. But because he was so good with helping me, I told him when Jennifer became old enough; I would have her do nice things for him. Andy was non-aggressive, non-violent, curious, quiet, and was a happy-go-lucky child while waiting for Jennifer to grow up. But Jennifer, on the other hand, was feisty, strong-willed, and always tried keeping up with her older brother who not only played with her; but looked after her too.

Things began to radically change when Andy started kindergarten! Andy found friends his age and only three houses from us. So, when Andy would go off to play with his new neighborhood friends, Jennifer didn't like it. She would follow him everywhere saying "Andy, mommy says you have to play with me." But of course this was why Andy's friends would say Andy, "here comes mommy says!"

Today, I think he looks up to her because she has so much wisdom. There is a strong bond with mutual admiration for each other. Andy is a natural engineer and can put anything together. Jennifer graduated in criminal justice, but when employment in her field was to no avail, she found her niche working in antiques at a prestigious store. It seems to keep her busy.

Our family was broken up in 1980, when our 23-year marriage ended in a divorce in Ypsilanti, Michigan. Hugh has since remarried, but I have remained single. I joined the Church of Jesus Christ of Latter Day Saints, and then moved to Seattle, Washington to be near my family. Andy was married, but is divorced and lives with his son Daniel Hugh Stults in Michigan. Jennifer's husband Charlie Hodge passed away on March 3, 2006. She and I both live alone in Sevierville, Tennessee but reside at different addresses. Besides church attendance, I joined the Red Hat Society and frequent the health food stores and Japanese stores to try and eat a healthy macrobiotic diet widely known as the healing diet.

Frank

He was shown favoritism as the youngest sibling with all the charisma. The rest of his siblings were always restricted and had to keep their noses to the "grindstone" by working on the farm. Frank was the only one to spend weekends with his friend Jack Hunnington who had parents "with means," and he would enjoy elaborate prepared meals at Jack's home; while the farm food was all we had and was quiet simple in comparison. People loved Frank because of his winsome personality, and he was also quiet handsome.

When W.W.II ended, the camp was closing with only Frank and I still left incarcerated in the Hunt Idaho Camp. We were given the opportunity to relocate to any place of our choice and we decided to join our sister Bessie in Rochester, Minnesota. Our train ride in 1945 meant we would be transferring trains in Omaha, Nebraska, at the largest train station in America. I wouldn't have been so fearful if I would have been able to distinguish the many little pit stops that were made along the way. But as it turned out, the train made numerous and numerous stops that kept me on edge and wondering if we should have gotten off each time the train would stop and start again.

Frank finally realized my uneasiness and would say that "he though we should have gotten off there!" That always frightened me, but I could soon tell he was trying to fool me. When we finally reached Omaha, it was a big relief for the attendant to tell us we would all disembark by leaving our suitcases on our train. That really troubled me again, but we were told we would be embarking on this same train but on a different train track by remembering the number of our train car. As a country girl with little confidence and Frank was a pillar of confidence, and I was so happy and relieved when we finally reached Rochester, Minnesota; Bessie was waiting to meet us there. When we all returned to Washington, Frank attended and graduated from the University of Washington with a CPA degree and also as a second Lt. in the Air Force. From his ROTC training at the University he went directly to the Macord Air Force Base in Tacoma, Washington.

He served in the Air Force as a uniformed officer, then a civilian in the Federal Civil Service. Rising to the position of Deputy Assistant Secretary of Defense for Audit, he was appointed by President Jimmy Carter to be Inspector General of the Department of Transportation. Later, President Ronald Regan appointed him to be Inspector of the Veteran's Administration. During that time, he also served as National President of the Japanese American Citizen's League (1984-86). He retired from government service in 1988 and now works for Deloitte, Haskins, and Sells as National Director of the Federal Audit Service. Today at the age of 78, he and his wife June Matsusawa live in Woodenville, Washington. They have 4 surviving children: Teresa, John, Gregory, and Glenn. John has followed in his father's footsteps by becoming a certified public accountant also.

The following pages are pictures located in Waikiki, Hawaii; these are pictures of the Memorial of the Famous 4 Divisions of the Japanese American Men who fought in the W.W.II.

The first top picture has four sides with plaques depicting the 4 Divisions and their insignia.

Located at the Fort DeRussy Park on KaLaKawa Ave. in Honolulu, Hawaii are these memorials honoring the Japanese American men who fought valiantly during World War II.

The Tenacity That Helped To Win Wodd War II

During World War II, the Japanese Americans were the 100 Infantry Battalion and the 442 Regimental Combat team. They were involved in the destruction of three of Germany's "impregnable" defense fortifications such as the Monte Cassino portion of the Gustav Line, the Apennine Mountain portion of the Gothic Line both in Italy and in the Vasques forests of Northeast France where the ferocious fighting took place. Each of these fortresses capitulated to Allied offenses which were designed to prevent Allied Advancement to Rome. Monte Cassino is where the Germans followed Hitler's orders for an all out defensive stand south of Rome. Following the Monte Cassino Operation, these American forces advanced to Anzio. By this time, after five months of continuous combat, the 100th Battalion had only 521 effective men remaining of the 1,300 originals who landed at Salerno. For the huge casualties the 100th sustained at Monte Cassino, the press dubbed it the Purple Heart Battalion.

The Gothic Line was composed of interconnected mountain defenses in Tuscany, including Mount Folgorito, which protected access to the Po Valley and the North. From this defensive fortress, the German's withstood allied attacks, for five months before the 442nd was recalled to Italy. In March of 1945 this operation from France, where they had just fought the enemy in the Vosques forests, helped to open the gateway for the 7th Army's invasion of the German Rhineland. On April 4,1945 the 442nd climbed the steep Mount Folgorito to see the mountaintop site where the men assembled the following morning and from where they mounted a full scale assault that broke the German Gothic Line in 32 minutes. This allowed the allies to pursue the enemy into the Po Valley and to the Italian Alps, where Germany surrendered.

The Final Aspects of World War II

Carrara is where the finest marble products are produced and Pietra-Santa is where in the spring of 2000, the local population, led by Dr. Americo Bugliani, a Java member built a monument to the Medal of Honor recipient Sadae Munemori to honor the allies for liberating Livornn(Leghorn), Italy. The allies major deep water port delivered heavy equipment and other materials to the allied forces in Pisa, the home of the famous leaning tower that was built in the 12th century. Tendola is where two memorials were built to honor the 442nd and at other sights.

MILITARY INTELLIGENCE SERVICE
"M.I.S."

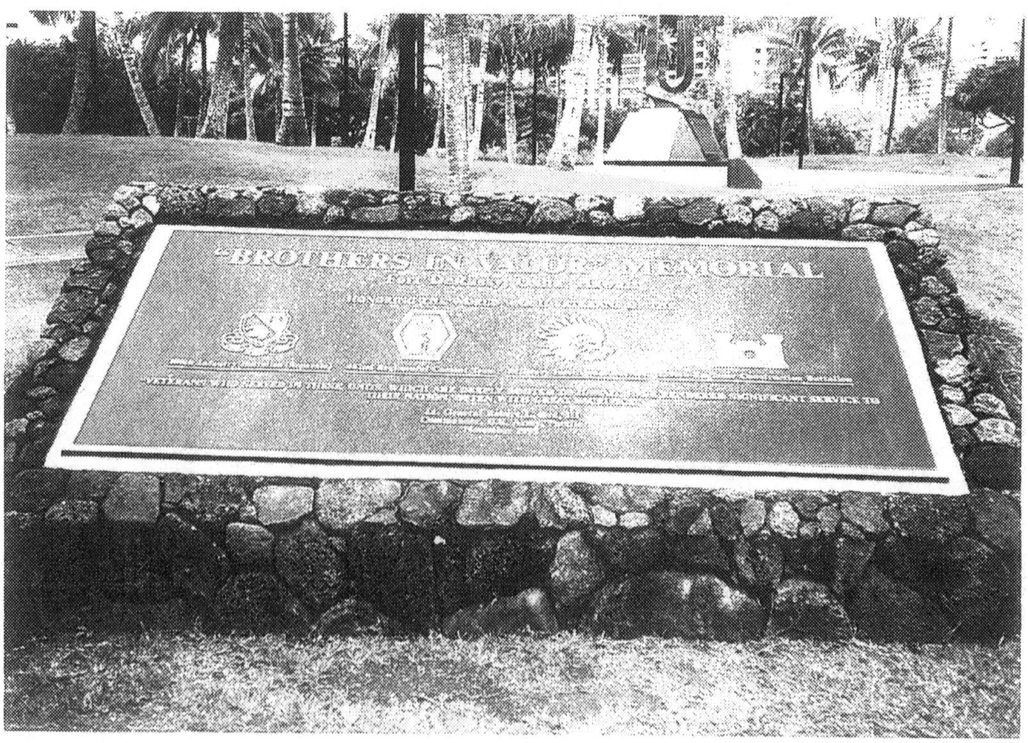
"BROTHERS IN VALOR" MEMORIAL

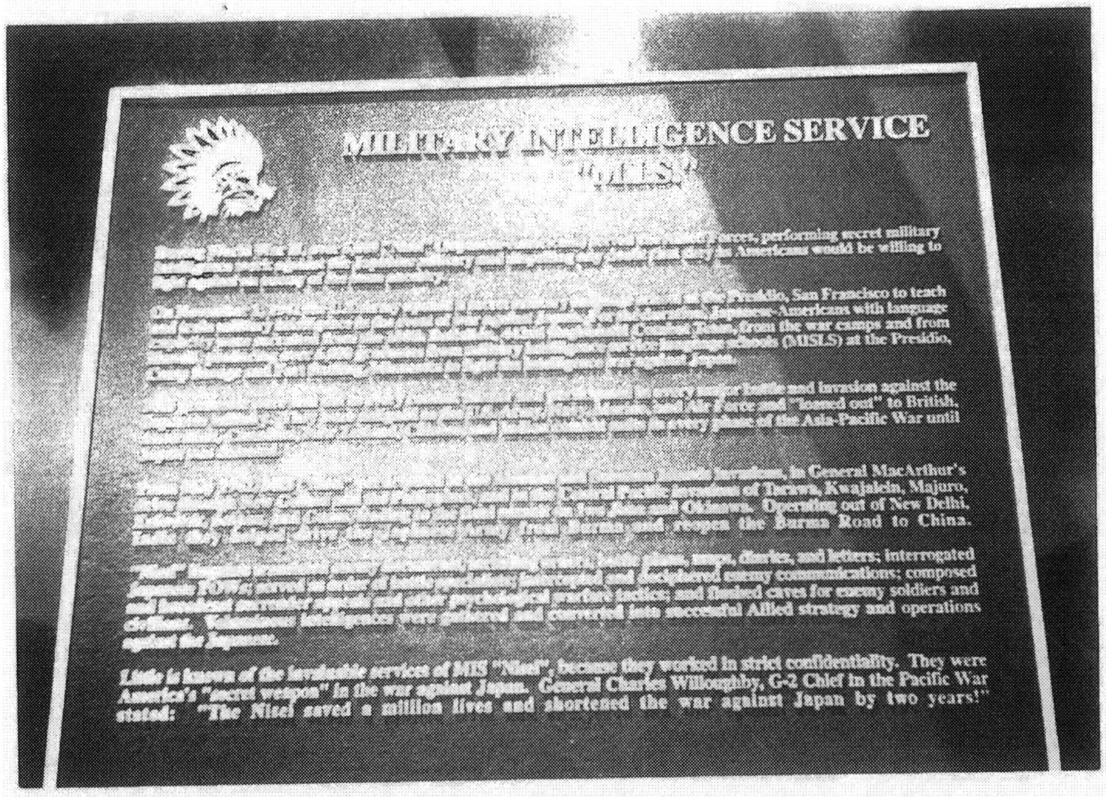
MILITARY INTELLIGENCE SERVICE
Little is known of the invaluable services of MIS "Nisei", because they worked in strict confidentiality. They were America's "secret weapon" in the war against Japan. General Charles Willoughby, G-2 Chief in the Pacific War stated: "The Nisei saved a million lives and shortened the war against Japan by two years!"

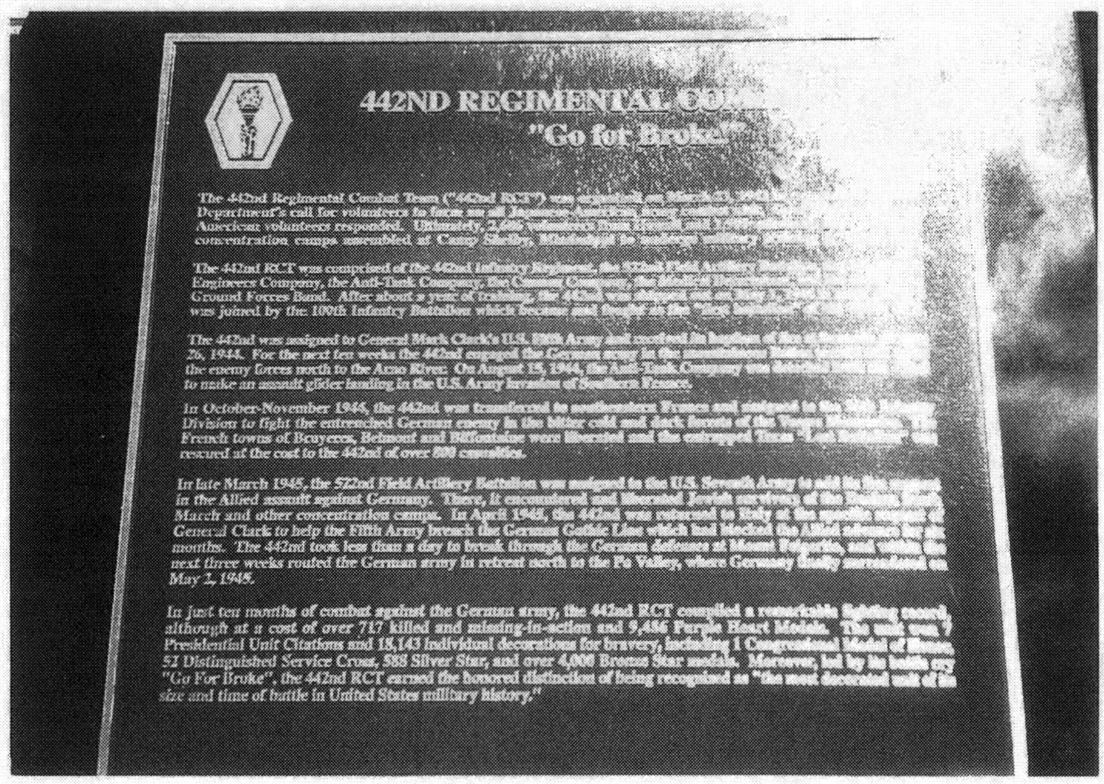
442ND REGIMENTAL
"Go for Broke"

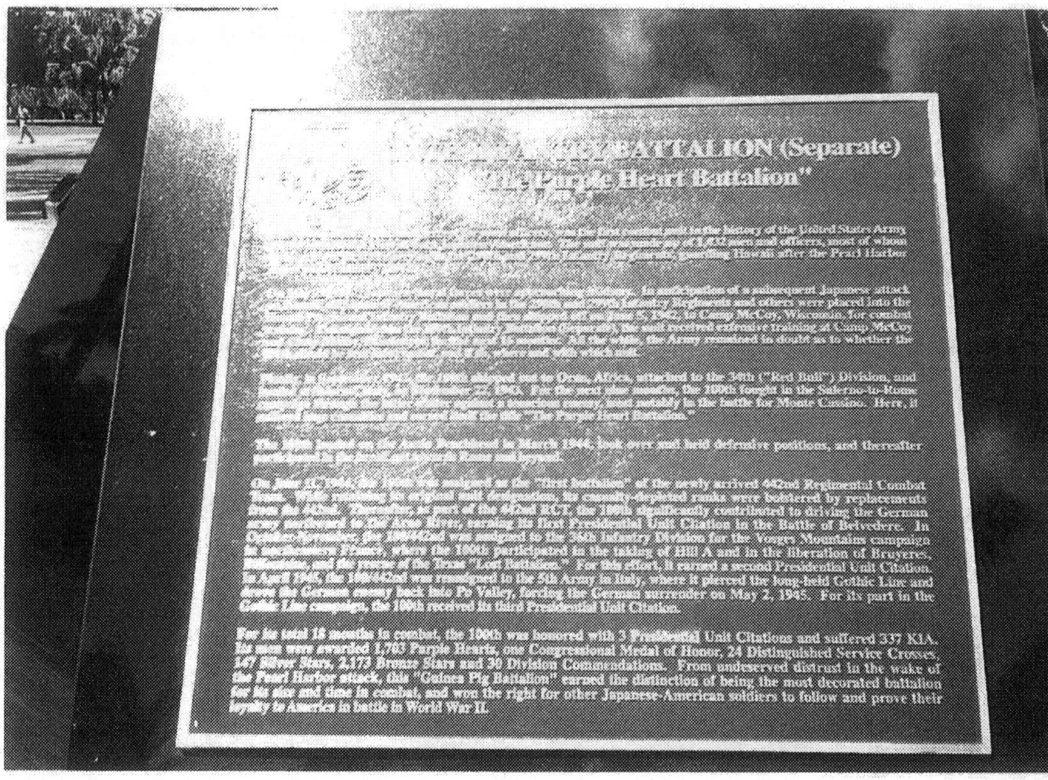
BATTALION (Separate)
"Purple Heart Battalion"
For its total 18 months in combat, the 100th was honored with 3 Presidential Unit Citations and suffered 337 KIA. Its men were awarded 1,703 Purple Hearts, one Congressional Medal of Honor, 24 Distinguished Service Crosses, 147 Silver Stars, 2,173 Bronze Stars and 30 Division Commendations. From undeserved distrust in the wake of the Pearl Harbor attack, this "Guinea Pig Battalion" earned the distinction of being the most decorated battalion for its size and time in combat, and won the right for other Japanese-American soldiers to follow and prove their loyalty to America in battle in World War II.

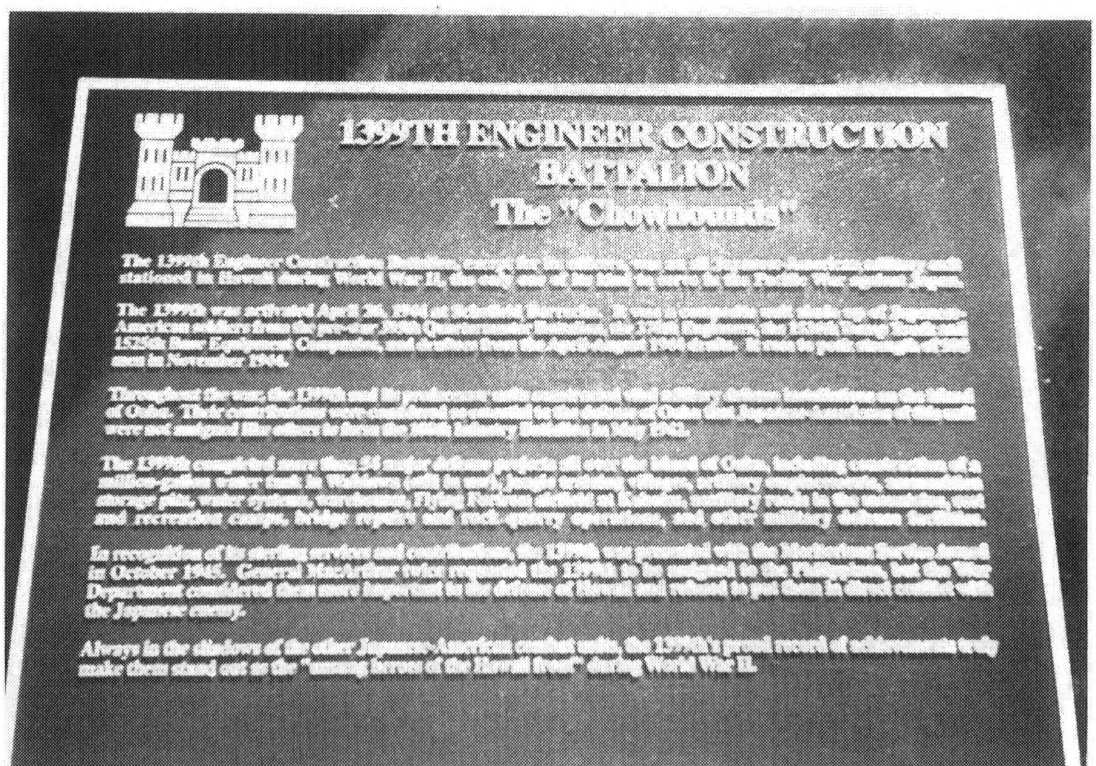
1399TH ENGINEER CONSTRUCTION
BATTALION
The "Chowhounds"

Vacationing to see Son John Hidemitsu Sato in Hawaii

Masamori and Masuyo at the Dole pineapple farm.

Masamori and Masuyo
Top: At their mini farm in Puyallup
Bottom: Masamori and Masuyo

Masamori's Autograph

CHAPTER 7

Prologue

The concept of the family crest in Japan is still alive and well today. Our identified history goes back to the beginning of the 12th century A.D. Generally, the family crests in Japan are called Ka-Mon with Ka meaning "family with their own genealogical trees" and Mon meaning "crest or emblem."

The History of Our Japanese Crests

In the early developing period of the samurai era, the Shimazu clan ruled over the entire southern Japan of Kyushu. The Shimazu Japo was the highest ranking position in the clan. They developed their own diamond crest that was used to distinguish themselves in battle. The Retainers ranked beneath the Japo and the Vassels as sub-Retainers.

The Genealogical Miracle

On September 14, 2010, Masamori's son Bob Satoshi Sato had passed away. The family learned about the genealogical story that came to light during the service held for Bob when his son, Stanley, spoke in honor of his father.

Twenty years before his passing, Bob had gone to Japan in an attempt to make a hand rubbing of Masamori's family crest. Due to the age of the crests, he was unable to do so. However, nine days prior to Bob's passing, his younger brother, Frank, had been in Japan and was able to accomplish Bob's efforts.

Frank's success came along through the help of a cousin Masako Sato. Because she resides in Kagoshima, Japan where Masamori was born and grew up, she was a big help to all the whereabouts and the locations. She took him to the Shimazu park where the Kinzan Machi cemetery is located in southern Kyushu, Japan. And, of course, it was where our family marker was located. Masako, also, informed Frank that her family had restored all of the crests and the monuments making it easier to make good hand rubbings of the original crest that date back to the 12th century.

It was a great timing to be there for Frank and a real blessing for all of us. The diamond crest is the basic clan Ka-Mon that appears on all the Sato monuments and there are many.

As a strong representative of his father, Stanley, had been searching into his family history. His interest intensified when his father inherited the one and only black silk robe called a haoli that his grandfather, Masamori Sato, brought back with him when he was returning to America from his maiden voyage back to Japan.

This robe has crests located at many areas on the haoli. However, the crests on his haoli all have added white rings surrounding the Shimazu diamond clan Ka-Mon. The rings surrounding the crests are not seen anywhere else. It makes me believe that Masamori's haoli was a special made presentation because of those special distinctive features added to the crest design.

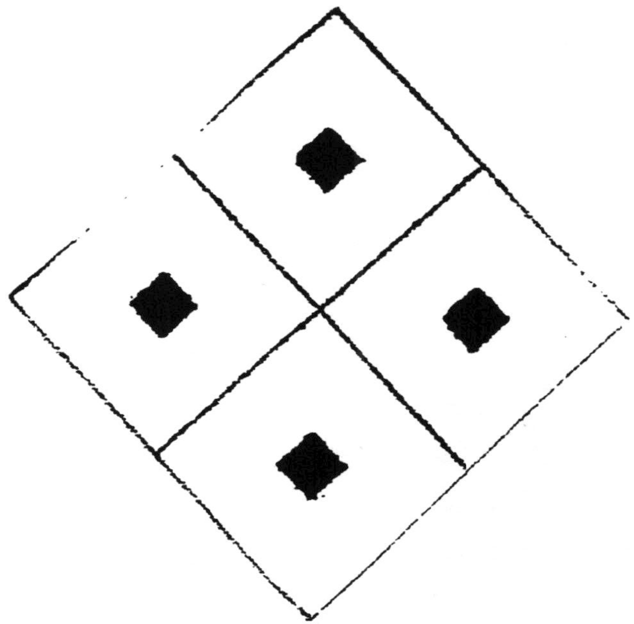

This is the original diamond Mon that belonged to the very first group of Samurais of the Shimazu clan when in conflict against other group clans. Each clan would distinguish themselves in the manner, during the 12th century, A.D. Masamori is a descendant of a SatoSamurai under the Shimazu clan.

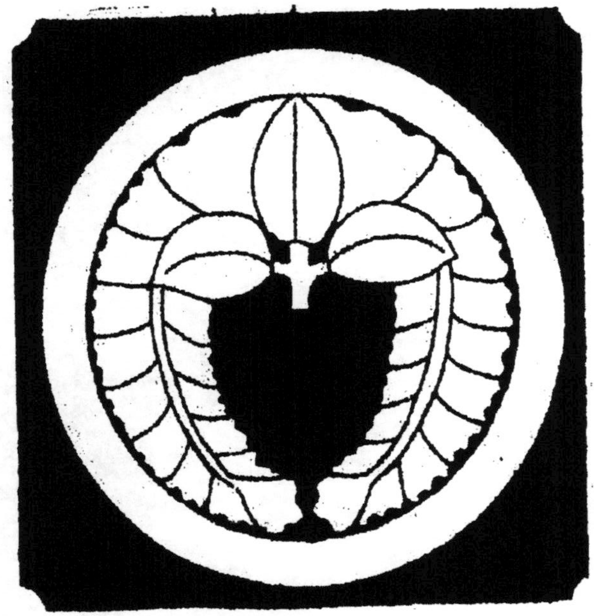

This is the Maru No Sagari Fujj Mon called the Weeping Wisteria design belonging to the Masamori Sato Family.

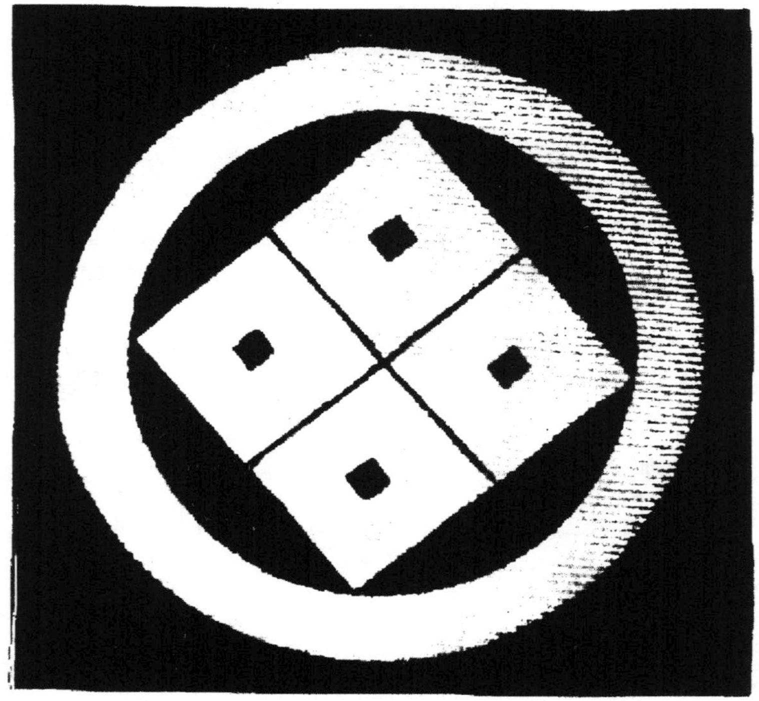

These Shimazu crests that are located in five areas of Masamori's haoli have an extra feature surrounding the original crest. The round ring around the crest must have been added to the haoli when they were painted on the haoli because this special feature has not been found anywhere else.

This is the front view of Masomori's Haoli.

Back of the Haoli.

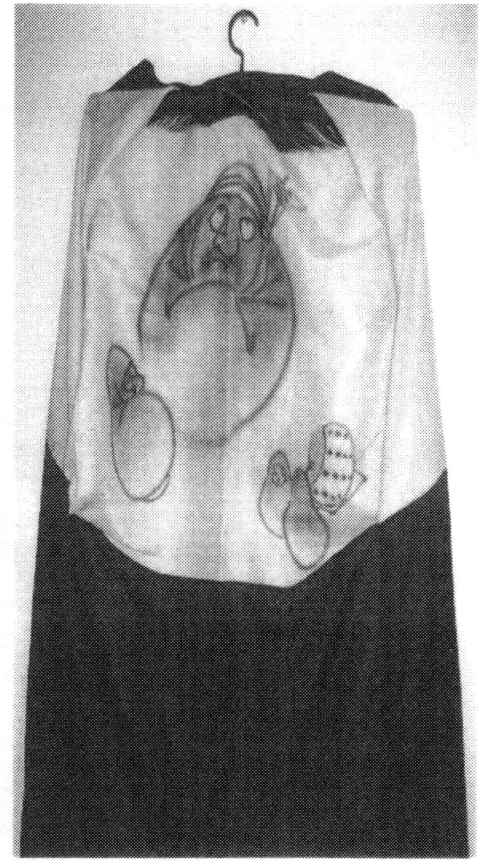

This is a facinating view of the inside back lining. It is a very special feature in the Haoli.

Both ot these views are actual hand rubbings of the Masamori Sato and his wife Masuyo (Ishikawa) Sato's family crests.

This is a combination crest of the Sato Samurai diamond crest at the bottom and with the wisteria Masamori design together.

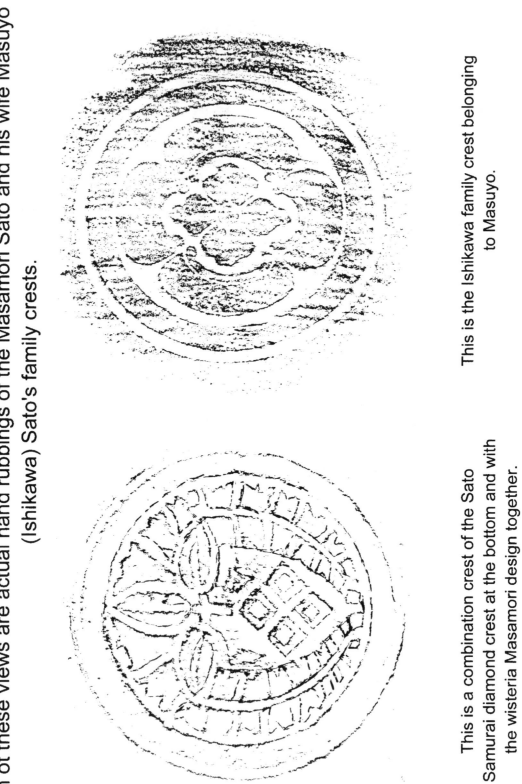

This is the Ishikawa family crest belonging to Masuyo.

Personal Comment

Masamori left the Minidoka Camp in 1944 and tended flocks of turkeys for a farmer near Wendell, Idaho until spring of 1946. Masuyo joined him in 1945. In 1946, they moved to a farm labor camp and worked on various farms in the Twin Falls area until 1947. Finally in November of 1947; Masamori and Masuyo and their youngest son Frank drove back to the West Coast. After a brief stay at the George Ota farm in Sumner, Washington; they established themselves on a one-acre lot and house in Puyallup, Washington in February of 1948. At the ages of 62 and 49, Masamori and Masuyo finally resumed a normal life working part-time at the neighboring George Richter farm, as well as on their raspberry farm. On September 14, 1953 they both became U.S. Citizens. In July of 1969, with old age and heart problems, they moved to Seattle to live with the oldest daughter, Betty.

Masuyo passed away on September 21, 1975 and Masamori on April 8, 1978. They are buried at the Washington Memorial Cemetery near the Sea-Tac Airport. The aspirations and enduring spirit of Masamori and Masuyo Sato, as Issei Pioneers, live on as a legacy to their children and to their adopted country.

I am very proud of the many accomplishments of Dad. My parents were model citizens. After two of their sons experienced service during World War II, the government finally and ultimately allowed them both their naturalized citizenship. In fact, for making it easier for them to take their citizenship test, the one time only tests were given in Japanese!

The Family Story

Frank has recollections about his father's formal black silk haoli as a child. He remembers the distinctive clan emblem located in many areas on the haoli when he wore it to various special occasions. The crest was also hand painted on the surface of a lantern that hung at the entrance of our home when we celebrated our Japanese ancestral memorial day.

And now, we have another Ka-Mon of a later period of time. The crest is called Mokkou (a round with weeping wisteria design) or (Malu no Sagali) in Japanese that belongs to Masamori's family. One hand rubbing from the cemetery was in combination of the original crest and the Masamori crest. Frank arranged to have pendants made for our family which are shown with other pictures in the later pages of the book.

Back, Author Rose Michiko Sato Stults
Front, Jennifer Lynn Stults and Andy Gene Stults

About the Author

Rose Michiko Sato Stults is the fifth child of six children born to Masamori and Masuyo Sato from Japan and originally from Sumner, Washington State. She was incarcerated with her entire family in 1943 at the age of 14 because of her national heritage; when President Franklin D. Roosevelt passed the Executive Order 9099.

The United States is comprised of universal countries and a "melting pot" of people. She and all of her sisters and brothers are also natural born citizens of the United States. She often recalled how her Chinese fortune cookies mentioned that she would do well through writings, but she never felt that was possible with her poor reading skills.

However, in the late years of her life in 1982; she went to Japan to search for mother's half sister Aunt Shizuko Fujii, she found out that Aunt Shizuko was full of some very interesting family history. Her brain became like a sponge as Aunt Shizuko told so many wonderful stories of the cultural and family history. Also, as a child she was computing her own father's stories that her siblings do not seem to remember.

Her inspirations came along with her interest in family history and genealogy. She felt that she had some important knowledge that needed to be passed on to everyone in the family. But most importantly, it would benefit her two adopted children who know so little about their heritage. This would also leave a wonderful legacy to all of our generations to follow.